Secrets of Smartphone Apps

Terms and Conditions

- 2 -

The Publisher has strived to be as accurate and complete as possible in the creation of this report, notwithstanding the fact that he does not warrant or represent at any time that the contents within are accurate due to the rapidly changing nature of the Internet.

While all attempts have been made to verify information provided in this publication, the Publisher assumes no responsibility for errors, omissions, or contrary interpretation of the subject matter herein. Any perceived slights of specific persons, peoples, or organizations are unintentional.

In practical advice books, like anything else in life, there are no guarantees of income made. Readers are cautioned to reply on their own judgment about their individual circumstances to act accordingly.

This book is not intended for use as a source of legal, business, accounting or financial advice. All readers are advised to seek services of competent professionals in legal, business, accounting and finance fields.

You are encouraged to print this book for easy reading.

Table Of Contents

Foreword

A good place to get ideas on phone apps is in social forums that target mobile users and developers. Many ideas as well as complaints are found in these forums. The complaints from users are great in terms of feedback as they will tell you what not to do with your app. Developers will also tell you what you should avoid when creating your app due to design complexity and programming tool restrictions. Most of these forums are free and you only need to register to participate in them.

Smartphone Apps Secrets

Chapter 1:

Synopsis

It is also a good idea to visit the websites of all the branded phones available on the market.

Discover Your App

You will notice on these sites that there is a tab for users to comment. If you click on the tab it will take you to another page where you will find visitor's comments and even complaints. You can even view posts that are archived. There are lots of ideas on new designs, software and apps for phones to be found. Just spend some time going through them.

Another avenue to get ideas is through social gatherings. When you are out with friends and associates, talk to them about their phones. Anyone who has bought a new phone will be more than willing to share the great features of their new phone. They also like to compare the features of different brands. They will tell you what new feature or apps their new phone has. They will also tell you what is good about the app, what is lacking in the app and what is not good about the app. All this info is great to have as it will give you insight into what is good, what is missing and what to avoid when designing an app for the mobile market.

Chapter 2:

Synopsis

For any type of business, a thorough market research is needed to tell you if the intended project venture is good or not. There are many sites that you can obtain market info and on many subjects. One such site is mobilephone development.com. It has great amounts of market research just on mobile phones and their apps. The research posted on this site is mostly done by big corporations which means that the data found on this site is valid and accurate.

Social Forums

Many ideas on phones and apps as well as complaints about them are found in social forums that target mobile users and developers. The complaints and comments from users are great in terms of feedback as it will tell you what not to do with your app, what not to buy, what brand is good and so on. Users and developers will also tell you what you should avoid when creating your app due to design complexity and programming tool restrictions. Most of these targeted social forums are free and you only need to register to participate in them.

Another avenue to get ideas is through focus group gatherings. These groups should be represented by age, gender, profession and other denominations. The analysis and results from these focus group gatherings will clearly show where your intended target group market lies. It will also show what type of app is popular, which brand of phone is the best with current models, how big is your intended market and what price level is acceptable. These focus groups will also tell you what is good about the app, what is lacking in the app and what is not good about the app. You will now have insight into what is good, what is missing and what to avoid when designing an app for the mobile market.

Chapter 3:

Be Different From Your Competitor's App

Synopsis

When you have performed a thorough market research, it will tell you what the market wants, what is available on the market and what you should do to penetrate the market.

Be A Leader Not A Follower

You have to adopt the Japanese mentality of how to penetrate the intended market. Take for instance, when the Japanese wanted to sell cars, they bought cars from Europe and the US and studied the cars. From the analysis, they concluded that they can make cars cheaper with the same accessories and features. They started manufacturing their own cars and marketed them worldwide. This is how Toyota, Honda and other Japanese brands emerged.

The defining factor for the Japanese was that they could give the same thing at a lesser price. The same can be said for any other product. If you sell any product that is similar to others in the market but is cheaper, you will penetrate the market and gain market share. Conversely, if you sell any product that has more user-demand features than your competitors, you will penetrate the market and gain market share. A great example of this is iPad. When it was launched, it was the first of its kind. It captured the whole tablet market until competitors caught up with cheaper models. Even now iPad maintains a large share in the tablet market, together with Samsung and Blackberry. The same scenario goes for iPod.

If price is constant, product differentiation becomes paramount in market acceptance. It is the logical choice for most people that when asked to choose between two cars of the same brand and model but one has more features, 100% of them will pick the one with more features.

Chapter 4:

Hiring Programmers With Extensive Experience

Synopsis

Once you have confirmed the design and functionality of your mobile app but are not qualified to program it, you need to find programmers with extensive experience to create the features that you want for the mobile market.

Seek Help When It's Needed

If your app is targeted for the Android market then the place to look for these programmers is globalemployees.com where they are a one stop center for outsourcing needs. They will handle all administrative functions in selecting experienced programmers that are tailored to your needs. They will:

- Find competent resources

- Manage infrastructure layout

- Check availability of software and hardware

- Labor & Employment Laws

- Holidays

- Appraisals

When hiring Android developers, you must ensure that they have the necessary skills to build really rich multimedia flash applications. They must have:

- Sound Knowledge of Android OS

- Experience in mobile & tab device applications

- The ability to conduct Android Testing

- Android Application Maintenance and Upgrade

India is a good source to get experienced programmers. The biggest advantage of hiring Android developers from India is that you spend almost 50% less on the resource as part of their salary, compared to their offshore western counterparts. Android developers in India are very versatile and they can provide Android application development on any platform namely Windows, Linux and Mac OS X. These developers in India are quite proficient in the English language, making communication with them easy. It is hard to explain the concept of the project to most people and even harder when there is a language barrier. In India the IT infrastructure is quite advanced, enabling clients to interact with their offshore locations by using the following options:

- Email

- Instant Messaging

- Skype

- Video Conferencing

With the above methods of communication, going through the design life cycle of the app for enhancements with the programmer on a constant basis is easy.

Chapter 5:
Building Your Apps For Different Types Of Smart Phones/OS

Synopsis

Once the design of your app has been decided, you also need to know which smartphone OS platform you want to integrate your app into. With so many on the market, it can be quite confusing. The market currently has the iPhone, the growing Android market, the Blackberry and Windows market. The logical choice would be to select the largest market. That would be the iPhone, followed closely by Android with Blackberry and Windows having small shares. Recent market surveys show that the Android has taken over the top spot with iPhone second and Windows a close third.

How to choose an OS

If the app's functionality is geared towards certain target groups like healthcare, law or financial services, then Blackberry and Windows are the logical choice as they have great penetration into these markets.

If the cost of creating the app for a specific platform is an issue then the Android platform is the logical choice. It is also the growing trend to develop apps for the Android platform. There are some problems on unique implementations with ActiveSync but these are likely to be ironed out soon.

However, when it comes to the actual development process, there are some who insist Android has the best development tools, database access and multitouch capability.

While some others point to Apple's emphasis on speed and reduced battery consumption, which means working without the bells and whistles of java or .net.

It is difficult to develop a corporate app [for iOS] that leverages external xml-based data repositories due to its lack of xml parsing. This means that it will take longer to write an app for iPhone than it will for Android or Windows. Longer programming time means more costs.

The above factors can assist in your choice of OS.

Chapter 6:

Synopsis

Mobile App development is progressively becoming one of the largest and quickest revenue generators for small and start-up technology companies globally. A new report pegs the mobile app revenue growth at $25 billion by 2015 (up from approximately $6.8 billion in 2010). It is estimated that more than 50 million apps will be downloaded by 2012.

Copyrights And Other Matters

Recently, with the spate of lawsuits and consumer complaints, legal protection and compliance are becoming important issues for mobile application development companies. The laws governing apps vary widely and are dependent upon the consumer base, nature of content, and the business model utilized for developing the apps.

Intellectual Property Right (IPR)

The IPR in the app software is a copyright that protects its authors the moment they write the code for the app. If the programming was done by the owners themselves, there is no issue with the IPR but if the ownership has been outsourced to a vendor, created through a joint effort, or derived from an open source software (OSS) then such copyright of the app might be complicated. Where all or part of the development of the app has been outsourced, the vendor agreement should stipulate clearly that the party financing the app development has acquired all IPRs to the software. It is also important to bind the vendor with a non-disclosure agreement (NDA) to ensure strict confidentiality while your app is being developed or you idea for the app might be sold to another party.

Where an app is developed through a partnership, each party owns the IPR only over the part of the app developed by it, in the absence of an agreement.

Chapter 7:

Selling Your Apps In Different Device Marketplaces

Synopsis

In order to sell your app, you have to define which OS it was developed to integrate with. There are several OS platforms in the market. There is the iPhone, the Android, the Windows and Blackberry. Once you have decided which platform to integrate your app with, you can only sell your app in the same platform that your app was programmed for.

Make Some Cash

Let us take a look at the Windows market, assuming that your app was programmed for this platform.

Once your app is completed, you can now sell it on Windows Phone Marketplace which deals in Windows phone apps. This marketplace handles all the billings and payments for you.

There are procedures which must be carried out before selling in the marketplace. These series of action are:

- Register as a Windows Phone Developer – register your application at App Hub. This is also the place for distribution of your app.

- Develop and Test Your Application – use Windows phone SDK to build your app. Design and prepare your app icon.

- Assemble the Prerequisites for Certification – upload your app to the marketplace in a .XAP file extension. This is an executable file.

- Submit Your Application for Certification – after uploading you have to certify your app. For submission, you can choose automatic publishing which publishes your application after certification. Your certification details are available on MSDN.

- Link to Your Application – once your application is published, it appears on Windows Phone Marketplace Catalog and you can promote the link of your app immediately.

- Updating Your Application – to update the version of your app, you need to update the users and also add your updated version in your membership account in Windows Phone Marketplace.

- Support – You can find support in App Hub in the form of community forums.

Chapter 8:

Building Apps With Advertising Opportunities

Synopsis

Since the 1990s, people have been predicting that the following year was going to be the year of mobile. Whether or not 2013 will turn out to be the year of mobile is anyone's guess, but the two things that are certain are that mobile has definitely gone mainstream and as a result, it's therefore an ad medium that any serious marketer has to take.

Mobile Ad Opportunity

In the US. there is a clear and present opportunity for advertisers to target mobile users through both mobile search and mobile app ad networks.

This has made it clear that it's not a question of whether you should be investing in mobile advertising. It's a question of how much you should be investing in mobiles.

In the US in 2011, Android and iPhones accounted for over 72% of all smartphones according to Nielsen's mobile report of which we see that search portals account for 3 of the 10 top destinations with Google topping the list for each.

According to Nielsen 49% of mobile consumers say they frequently use their smartphones while shopping or when they are away from home. That's half of mobile users who use their phones while they're in a purchasing mindset or commercial environment.

These users are probably looking for reviews and price comparisons and for the price-competitive retailers, that's a significant opportunity to target users who are not only interested in your products, but are ready to buy if the product's price is right.

Smartphone users spend more time using apps than on the web. Nielsen has reported that Android users spent more than twice the amount of time using apps than they did on the mobile web.

Chapter 9:

Implementing The Free Marketing Model – Create A Lite(Give For Free) And Full Version(Paid)

Synopsis

The marketing of apps is no more different than any other product. These days, when any new product is launched, the common marketing strategy is to get customers to try out the product. Most users are creatures of habit and familiarity. They usually stick to a particular brand even though there are another 12 different brands on the shelf. They have used it and know what it does and are used to it.

Free Trials

The marketing of a new app is the same. There are dozens of apps with similar features on the market. So trying to get users to try them is a challenge, let alone buy them. An app with a free trial will stand a better chance of being sold than one that does not have a free trial. A free trial is also good because it benefits both the user and the app owner. The user gets to use the app without fear or failure while the owner of the app has made half a sale. While the user is using the app, he will find that there are certain limitations to this free version. If he likes the app and its features then he would probably buy the full version without hesitation. The user knows that the app suits them after using the free version. Without a free trial, users are in a state of hesitation about the unknown. Free versions eliminate product uncertainty. The owner of the app, on the other hand also benefits. They know that if their app does what it is supposed to do and that they have based their app on market research, then the chances of users buying the full versions are good. No free versions, no sale.

Chapter 10:

Expanding Your App To The Web – Allow Synching/ Social Platform Or Etc

Synopsis

The Web has changed the way people communicate on a daily basis. Without the support, resources, and insight of family, friends, colleagues, mentors and business contacts, our lives would be very different. There are now more ways than ever to make connections and stay in contact using your app.

Social Apps

There are many mobile social apps available that are free. The following are some of the popular ones on the web.

Twitter – Twitter is all about real time reporting or commenting. People tweet on the spot, what is happening and when it's happening. Twitter is the #1 microblogging service app you can have on your phone. Share and discover what's happening right now, as it happens, in world events, private events, or unusual events.

Skype – You can stay in contact with anyone who is also on Skype on their mobile, computer or tablet.

Fring – This app is similar to Skype with the exception that you can make calls from a Fring user to another Fring user for free through the web.

My Space - This started out as a space for bands and their fans to communicate and has grown to make room for everyone. You can promote your band, discover new music, meet people, or just express yourself in any way you choose. MySpace is easy to use, and even easier when it's on your phone.

WhatsApp – This app is a free texting service from mobile to mobile using the web. So that means that there is no charges incurred for the texts. You can text anyone who has WhatsApp anywhere in the world.

StumbleUpon – This app is a search engine for finding interesting, amusing websites. You can also make friends while using it.

Wrapping Up

Designing and launching a new mobile app can be difficult, but with the proper guidance and tips it will be much simpler. Creating a new app is also a great way to dray in money as the mobile app market is booming. All you need is a fresh idea and a way to put it out there and you are sure to tap into this exploding market! What are you waiting for, get started now! I wish you the best of luck!

www.ingramcontent.com/pod-product-compliance
Lightning Source LLC
LaVergne TN
LVHW050305200726
843509LV00015B/3163